All Scripture references taken from the KJV of the Holy Bible, unless otherwise indicated.

The Robe, *Part I*

by Dr. Marlene Miles

Freshwater Press 2023

ISBN: 978-1-963164-15-2

Table of Contents

The Robe

Part I,

The Lessons of Joseph

Father, we thank You for this word today. We thank you for taking us from where we are, with what we know about Joseph, even lessons that we've learned in Sunday School and enlarging us, building precept upon precept, line upon line, and giving us revelation, and knowledge that we may grow and grow up in You.

Lord, may You be glorified as Your Kingdom is built, in Jesus' Name, Amen.

Israel Loved Joseph More

Now Israel loved Joseph more than all his
children because he was the son of his old age.
And he made him a coat of many colors.
(Genesis 37:3)

Now Israel loved Joseph more than all his children because he was the son of his old age, and he made for him a coat of many colors. Historian, Josephus Flavius says that Jacob was blessed with his sons; by his sons, was he blessed.

Jacob had ten boys prior to Joseph, by his wife, Leah and two handmaidens. Jacob's sons blessed him because his boys were full of virtues; deficient in nothing. As we look closer, we'll see they were leaders. Jacob's sons were the leaders of the tribes of Israel. These boys had virtues…, they were mighty men of valor, and they had skills. They had the abilities, such as Issachar could discern the times. The Tribe of Benjamin was ambidextrous. These people were skilled with weapons. They had many skills, these ten boys.

But Joseph was the son of Jacob's old age, and he was his favorite. Historians say that Joseph was good looking. He was virtuous of mind. Something else of note about Joseph that made him a particular favorite of Jacob's, and that was that he excelled in prudence over the rest. Prudence is common sense. He was wise in handling matters. He used good judgment. He handled himself well. Jacob's boy, Joseph was a steward; that is a person who manages well.

So, Jacob, with all of these boys, and even being the son of Isaac, who was the son of Abraham, certainly he knew how to dress his boys. He knew how to dress Joseph. He knew how to clothe and attire all of his kids, so he made Joseph a coat of many colors. That coat of many colors was spiritually symbolic.

In Bible times to make colors, dyes are used. Dyes are made from precious pigments in the Earth and in stones that are ground up and mixed in solutions. Dyes were very expensive. Remember Lydia in the Old Testament? She was a trader in purple. She was a very well-off woman and she supported ministries in the times of Jesus, and the disciples who became the apostles. She was a supporter of Christianity in the early days,

More expensive dyes were used for royalty. Joseph's coat was very symbolic in a way that we will discuss. As said, colors are very expensive. God could have made each and every one of us the exact same as with a cookie cutter mold, but He didn't. He made the investment into colors, shades, hues. He made us red, yellow, black, olive, brown and every kind of variation in between. He made us of many colors. Look at yourself. God took the time; He made the investment in you to make you the color that you are. Aren't you gorgeous? Yes, all to His Glory.

This is how the coat of many colors was spiritually symbolic.

And they sang a new song saying that. To take the book, and to open the seals thereof. For thou was slain, and has redeemed us to God by that blood out of every kindred, and tongue, and people and nation. (Revelation 5:9)

The colors on that coat were representative of every kindred and tongue and people and nation; and that's who's going to be around the Throne of God. That's who's going to be saying that He is worthy. Worthy is the Lord--, all people. Not just one race, not just one denomination, one, not just one culture of people, but many kindred, tongues, peoples, and nations.

Joseph, the favorite of his father, was beginning to have a spiritual awakening. He was getting dreams and visions from God. Joseph was sharing these with his family, and they were discerning what these dreams meant. They were realizing that Joseph was also favored of God. He was well chosen of God because he had a certain destiny, a certain future that was awaiting him.

The brothers probably despised Joseph even before the dreams because Joseph had a different parentage than they had. Rachel, who was Jacob's favorite wife, was the mother of Joseph and of course one other, Benjamin, who is not brought into this just yet. The older boys were sons of Aunt Leah and sons of the handmaidens, Bilhah and Zilpah.

Handmaidens didn't make it so well in that family. Remember Abraham and Hagar? A handmaiden could be sent away if she displeased the real wife or anyone in the house for that matter, so handmaidens' kids probably kept quiet, for the most part.

As said, Joseph was hearing from God. He was having dreams and probably seeing some visions. God was showing Joseph his future, about his identity, about his purpose, and his destiny. God can speak in many ways, but dreams were how He was speaking to Joseph.

God was only talking to Joseph about this matter, and Joseph invited his family into the interpretation and discussions about the dreams. Joseph involved his family, God didn't. God could have given the dream to Jacob and told Jacob to pick which boy, but **God** picked which boy. God picked which child. He could have just given the dream to another member. But **God** chose Joseph and sent him night visions.

There he was, almost the baby at the time--, I've been that young before, haven't you? Joseph was having a spiritual awakening, and possibly thinking that everyone else around him must already be walking in their spiritual purpose. They must have already had theirs because of their age. They must have already been so excited to begin to hear such wonderful things about their future from God. Joseph wasn't even alive when some of those boys were his current age.

Many families have a wide range of ages with their children, especially when there's more than one mother, or more than one father, but definitely when there is more than one mother.

Having multiple parents is polygamy and polygamy begets witchcraft. You don't believe it? What do you think was happening to Joseph, even at the hands of his brothers? Evil imagination and the willingness, the gall to carry it through **is** witchcraft.

So, Joseph believed that his family was going to be so happy for him. He believed that they were already walking with the Lord and now he finally was going to be growing up, getting his life's assignment from God. Joseph really thought they would be happy for him.

I've been that young before, haven't you? I have thought just because I was happy about something, a favor that I was getting or a special opportunity that I was getting, that other people were going to be happy for me. That other people in my *family* were going to be happy for me--, that other people in my church family were going to be happy for me.

Didn't they have the same daddy? If they have the same relationship with God, then they have the same Daddy, spiritually. In the church, aren't we all supposed to have the **same** Father? Aren't we supposed to be brothers and sisters, in the Kingdom no matter our natural parentage?

Jacob was everyone's natural dad in that family, and Joseph surely believed that they had already experienced their *dreams* so they'd be happy to see him, coming of age, spiritually speaking. Well, I used to think like that too. You know, when I was *that* young.

When those in a family--, a natural family or a church family do not have the same parentage, that is polygamy. And polygamy is the beginning of witchcraft. It is said that polygamy makes for the worst form of witchcraft. There is parental witchcraft and sibling witchcraft as we see in these chapters regarding Joseph.

Even in a church?

Ye are of your father the devil, (John 8:44).

It depends on what *spirits* are in a person indicates the spiritual *parentage* of that person.

Whomever a person listens to and obeys is their *parent*.

Joseph's brothers were jealous of his anointing, and they were jealous of his dream. They were jealous of his parentage--, same daddy, different moms. They were jealous of his future. They were jealous of the power and the position he was going to hold according to Joseph's dreams from God.

But, they never doubted God, did they? They believed that these things would come to pass, but they didn't want Joseph to have that destiny. If they didn't believe that those things would come to pass, they would never have hated Joseph, they would have just laughed at him and mocked him.

The Prophetic Dream

Genesis 37:20, reads, Joseph's brothers despised his dreams, which means they hated his future; they hated his destiny.

When God gives you a dream or speaks to you in any of the ways that He can speak to you, when He gives you a prophetic word, it may mean that you **need** a glimpse into the future. In Joseph's case, it was going to be harder; God knew that Jospeh's brothers would fight him and fight this destiny.

We all know that the other brothers had amazing destinies. Perhaps they had no prophetic visions into their destinies so even though they were gifted and blessed by God, they chose to fight their younger brother. When needful, God gives you a picture of the end, so you'll know what the puzzle is going to look like when all the pieces fit together.

Rejoice when you get a prophetic word or vision or a dream from God. But you may be getting that preview into your destiny because it's going to take a long time to get there, or because it's going to be arduous.

Therefore, those brothers should never have been jealous. You should never be jealous of anyone for those reasons, either. When God gives you a dream, it's nobody's place to hate it. And if they do, they should take it up with God. They shouldn't despise you because God gave it to you. God is the giver of dreams, purpose, anointing, destiny, and gifts, and He gives them to whomever He chooses. We have no say in whom He gives what to.

Yet, when you tell your dream to family members or close associates, you figure you're telling it to likeminded folk. I used to be that young before. Discern every *spirit*. Cast not your pearls to swine. Don't let people talk you out of things that you know the Lord is talking you into. And if the Lord has to lead you a step at a time, it's probably not going to be as easy as the guy who doesn't get previews or have to get one or more prophetic dreams or visions into his future.

Joseph's Dreams

You've been hearing about Joseph's dreams probably since Sunday School. I'm just going to give you the line upon the line that you already have. I'm going to give you the precept upon the precept that you already have, I'm going to give you the revelation. By the Word of God, by the Spirit of God, and we will build upon the revelation that you already have. And then we will go from glory to glory.

Remember, the sheaves were all bowing to Joseph, and then the moon and the stars were all bowing to him as well. And so Joseph was relaying these dreams and he was the center of these dreams. At that time Joseph was 17 years old. What is he supposed to think? How self-centered is the average teenager? Even a 17-year-old, the world revolves around them, so they think.

If you get a dream or a vision from God and you are the center of it, you need to check because it may not be from God. But if your dreams, purpose, or workplaces you as the focus or as the primary, it's still of God. As long as God is at the center of this, Jesus is at the center of it and it is in divine purpose.

If you got a dream or vision and you don't see God at the center of it, then look for purpose. When you see Godly purpose, you will see God. When you see the future in it, you see God. When you get or see a generational blessing, you'll see God.

God will bless so that it is easy to live in the *overflow* of the blessings that God has for you. For example, if you believe you receive a vision from God, that He's going to make you a big-time celebrity, movie star, that's your flesh. That's not God. That's the stuff that fairy tales are made of. But if God shows you how you will become XYZ in the Kingdom and how you can bless and be a blessing, now that's God. And when your dream is for others and for other people groups, especially kindreds, tongues and nations, anytime you have to leave your own comfort or place of your birth, like Abraham had to do, that is of the Lord.

Speaking of fairy tales, we need to be careful because visions of grandeur and fame can also come from the devil. The devil also gifts people and gives them money, status, fame based on some evil covenant and evil trade he has made with them. So--, just because you have a vision or see a future of thus and so, make sure you are getting it from God, through Jesus Christ, else you may be selling your soul. Hell was never designed for man and no human is supposed to end up there. But soul-sellers, beware because without repentance, and forgiveness in Jesus Christ, Hell is the final destination, the last stop.

Full of Virtues

Both Joseph and his brothers were full of gifts. They were full of virtues; they were full of good things from God. God had blessed them that way. And he blessed Jacob by blessing him with the sons who were a blessing.

The Word says to covet the best gifts. Did the brothers look on Joseph and decide that his gifts were the best and they wanted his? The gift that God gives you, the gift that works in you and through you, in for others, is the best gift for you. Someone else's gift may not work through you. It may not work for you. It may not work for others because you're not supposed to have your hands on that.

One fateful day, the 10 older boys were out tending sheep. They were supposed to be in a town called Shechem, but they were not there. Joseph found them in Dothan. Their father had sent Joseph, so it was just the boys there, no dad.

Envying his destiny, Joseph's brothers decided this day they would get rid of Joseph. They despised his future. They despised his destiny. They despised the favor that the Lord was planning to bestow upon Him, and they decided to get rid of Joseph, so they put him in a well.

While in the well, Joseph may have been thinking, *Hey, wait a minute, I'm too gifted to be down in this well.*

David could have been thinking the same thing as he was hiding in the caves from Saul. *I'm too gifted and anointed to be here.*

Moses, when he was in the desert, or Elijah when he was hiding from Jezebel could have been thinking the same thing: *I'm too gifted for all of this.*

What about you? You're too gifted to be hidden, aren't you as well? Doesn't the word say to let your light shine? Doesn't the Word say don't hide it under a bushel?

You're too gifted of God to be hidden away or stuffed away anywhere.

By definition, gifts are things that are *given*. If what you have is not given, it is not a gift--, it is a possession. If you keep what you discern as gifts for yourself, for personal use, only, they are not gifts.

Gifts from God are not for private treasure to heap upon your own lust. This affords another clue as to whether the gift *is* from God or not. *Who is it for? Is it for someone other than yourself?* Then it is most likely from God. (If Joseph with his stewardship gift had amassed all that could and hoarded it for himself to become very powerful in an evil way – that is a perversion of God's gift. The devil will be all in it.)

You're gifted, and you probably are too gifted to be in the situation that you're in. You're gifted, with the gift that you have, but God is not just giving the gift *to* you. When you're gifted, that means you have much to give to other people.

You're like a cargo ship, heavy laden, and that ship is gifted with gifts to drop off at various destinations. It's not just to sail around the oceans for 50 years, full of cargo and seeking to get more and more and more.

For example, it is not just a heap degrees for yourself so you could be smarter, smarter, smarter. It's not just so you can get more positions within the church--, getting more keys and more titles, but your gifts are things to be given out.

God has to give you a gift because without God, you don't even have an offering to bring Him unless He gives you one. When it's Father's Day, you don't have a gift, unless as a child, unless your mother gives you a gift to give to your father. You came into the world naked, like all of us, you came with nothing. Therefore, unless the Lord gives you a gift, you have no gift to give to anyone.

Spiritual giftedness is God sending gifts to people by you. The spiritual gifts that you have is God sending gifts to other people, *by* you.

I grew up in rural America, in the country, and the nearest corner store was 10 miles away from our house. So, when somebody went to the store they *sent by* other people. Everybody on the whole street didn't need to go to the store very often. They'd go for weekly shopping yes, but for odds and ends, we might just *send by* someone else. A kind friend, relative or neighbor may say, *"I'm going to the store, do you want anything? Do you need anything?"*

My mom might give that neighbor the money for and say, *I would like you to bring me a pound of butter and a gallon of milk.*

This type of favor is reciprocated a lot in the country and among good neighbors.

God sends things by people a lot. If God wants Sister Sally to have such and such a gift today and He knows you are going to see or spend time with Sister Sally, He may *send by* you. He will send that gift within you and anoint you so that gift will work *through* you, for you to give it to Sister Sally. For instance, if Sister Sally is going through a hard time and she needs a certain Fruit of the Spirit, perhaps she needs goodness--, she needs somebody to be good to her, either because either she's acting out and she needs from and the model goodness to her. Maybe she's been gossiping a lot, and you go there with your goodness, and turn the conversation to praying for the person she was gossiping about, rather than just gossiping about them.

Perhaps Sister Sally is not gossiping, and she's been really good to folk lately, so now as a sowing and reaping thing; she has goodness coming to her. But, there's no one in her immediate circle to be good to her and you are going to spend time with Sister Sally today. So, God *sends by* you. He sends the gift, the spiritual gift. The Fruit of the Spirit--, Goodness within you stirs it, quickens it, brings it to life for you to give to Sister Sally. Hallelujah.

God knows you're going to go see someone, He says, *Oh, let me send something by you, let me send it by you.* It is not always happenstance or by the way. All through the Bible God sent people where He needed them to go to do what He needed them to do.

Many times, we don't know who to go to, or what to take or how to give it to them, unless the Lord tells us. Jonah going to Ninevah comes to mind. God was sending salvation, or the opportunity to receive salvation to Ninevah by Jonah, but Jonah decided he was going to go in the opposite direction. It's not our place to decide who's going to get the gift that God says they're supposed to have. If you need to take time to repent, if God told you to give something to someone or to do something for someone and you have not because you personally don't like them like Jonah didn't like the people in Ninevah, this might be your time to repent.

God Sent Gifts

Another person that God *sent by* was Jesus. As Jesus came to Earth, He brought salvation and redemption with Him. God sent His Word to heal us.

The spiritual gifts you have are not for you. It's more like you're the FedEx guy, the postmaster, and Brown all rolled into one. You are to be delivering gifts from God to people. And like Joseph, when you deliver, you bring deliverance.

Your dreams and destiny involve you giving the gift and the gifts that the Lord gives you. It's called your ministry. We are God's hands and feet and vocal cords in the Earth. We are the Body of Christ. If God wants so and so to have such and such, He will *send by* someone to ensure that so and so gets such and such. Someone is sent to a desired place, to a desired person, to a designated individual, family, or group of people, to give the gift that God has *sent by* them.

The *University of Through*

The gift is from God, *through* you. Not to you, not for you, not because of you, but through you. Not from you. It's not even about you, but it's *through* you. Any of us could take a course in *through you*, at the *University of Through.*

In life, we go *through,* we pray *through*, and we should always endeavor to see things through. However, it's not about you or <u>for</u> you; it's through you. Spiritual gifts come *through* you. The Fruit of the Spirit manifests in you, but people receive of that Fruit, through you. Spiritual gifts come *through* not just <u>**to**</u>. Not to you, not of you, not by you, but through you.

If you think, *Hey, I walked in the room and this happened, and that happened.* No, you didn't.

You walked in the room and **<u>God</u>**, who had *sent by* you came *through* you to change the circumstances, the situation or the individuals in that room. The *University of Through* is not the university of you.

Therefore, your dream or vision about the gift is usually instruction on how to, when to, and where to take the gift. God didn't just give you gifts just for you. He didn't let you sing like that just so you can entertain yourself or make a whole bunch of money.

He didn't allow you to discern *spirits* just so you can see (and say) what's wrong with people. Do something for these people; pray for them!

God didn't give you the gift of a big fat bank account just to count your money. Probably, like Lydia, you're supposed to be a supporter of ministry. Some people--, that's their whole ministry--, to be a supporter. They may not have another spiritual gift, but they have a way of accruing money and wealth to be a blessing. They have the gift of giving. That could be your ministry. So don't force something else if that is your ministry.

Not only that, money with no purpose to it will sooner or later be corrupted. That's why demonic money destroys people sooner or later. Be sure to put your God-given money to Godly purposes so that money won't be corrupted.

When you fully understand that your dream, your anointing, your gifting, your purpose is for other people, you get it, and that's *through* you. You've just graduated from the *University of Through.* Congratulations.

Demotions

Joseph was sold into slavery by his half-brothers who were trying to demote him from the family. You can't demote anybody from a family. God decides family. Mom and Dad get married, and under the covenant of Holy Matrimony, which is sanctioned and ordained by God, that covenant breeds life, and creates a family.

Evil covenants breed death. The devil comes not but to steal, kill and to destroy. Any covenant that includes the devil will end up in untimely loss, destruction, and death of something, and/or someone. Not to scare you but it is possible, even while married, depending on how conception occurs that God may not be all in it… (that's another whole book). So, always be prayerful when you are with your spouse, especially when trying to conceive.

Within the Godly covenant of marriage, God decides family. You have no say so in who your brother is, who your sister is, and the natural or spiritual for that matter. So, stop trying to run people out of your natural family.

Stop trying to run people out of church. Stop trying to run out of churches, trying to avoid *those* people. Your brother or sister really is none of your business. Just obey God and his delegated authority and do what you're told to do.

Jesus asked His Disciples, ***"Who is my mother and my brother?"*** And, then He answered, ***"Whosoever will do the will of God."***

Now that sounds like a loophole to me because if you think that someone in your circle or in your church is sinning you don't want to have anything to do with them. But pay attention here: Whosoever will do the will of God, you see, that's a two-parter. The *will* of whoever will do the **will** of God is whoever is doing it now. And it also means whoever *will* in the future do the will of God. You see, God is drawing as He sees fit, from even the multitude, with loving kindness and He is not confined by Time.

He drew you. Nobody believed, after all that running around you did, that you would end up in a church serving the Lord, but God took you out of the Multitude.

We are all born in sin, even within the covenant of holy matrimony --, we are not born saved. We are born into the Multitude. We are shaped in iniquity the Word says.

So now that we are saved, couldn't you now draw somebody else?

You must prophetically believe that God can and will draw anyone whosoever that He will--, even from the Multitude. And whoever will do the **will** of God.

Jesus had brothers and sisters; He didn't choose who they were, and Joseph had one sister, and 11 brothers, but he didn't get to choose who they were. You got a problem with your siblings, then you need to take it up with God.

The Word also says that those from our own household will be our enemies. Well, a close enemy is far worse than one afar off, so we have to be wise and still not fight against flesh and blood. We need to pray and war *spiritually* in these matters. Your siblings, relatives, born into sin just like you were, may choose to stay that way and continue being influenced and "parented" by the devil.

When siblings or people who are living in the same house, or close together, but they have different parentage, that is polygamy. And polygamy fosters witchcraft. Witchcraft makes even siblings and relatives into enemies. There does not have to be polygamy to have household witchcraft. Sibling rivalry may naturally occur, or it may be incited by parental favoritism--, even if the parents are not aware that they are playing favorites.

Therein is the source of many family battles and problems. Therein was the problem in Joseph's family but being put in a pit then later sold into slavery, witchcraft looks like it was going to be the cause of the end of Joseph.

Witchcraft is not a plaything. When evil imagination is sparked and the devil finds out that you are willing to go all the way, Satan is now in an evil covenant with you, and he's out for blood. The demonic anointing on your original plans, if it wasn't unto death before, it will transform into that by the devil. In Joseph's case, Reuben said, *Let's not kill him*. But as time went by, and those boys sat and ate the lunch that JOSEPH brought them, while Joseph languished in a pit, showing that they had seared consciences. Once the devil sees that, the plan can escalate into more evil.

Conscience or no--, you cannot demote anybody from a family. They are still going to be your brothers, your sisters, and your mother and father's children no matter what. Your mom can't kick them out of the family. Your dad can't kick them out. They will still have the same blood. Cain tried to kick Abel out of the family of Adam and Eve, by killing him, but, even dead, Abel's blood was crying out from the grave. Abel was still a member of that family and still in the family of God. As far as God is concerned, Abel was still a part of that family. It's exactly why we are still repenting for the sins of our ancestors. They ae dead and gone to us, but not out of the bloodline, according to God.

If evil overtakes a person and they denounce God and join up with Satan, they themselves can defect from the Kingdom of God, else no other witchcraft or evil can pluck them out of God's hands. Worse, if they were related to you, you now have witchcraft or occultism in your bloodline, but they are still in your family. Are you your brother's keeper? Yes, in the sense that you should care that they are saved for themselves and for the impact it will have on the family bloodline.

Even if you form some type of a clique' or alliance with some other disgruntled siblings and agree on it like Joseph's brothers did, you can't kick them out. That's a soulish prayer in which soul ties are formed. They are very unacceptable to the Lord because the devil is in every evil soul tie.

Joseph's ten brothers made an evil soulish agreement. It is amazing to me that in the 17 years Joseph was gone, while their very old father was grieving, not one of them blurted out that they had sold Joseph, their father's favorite into slavery. I worry that if Jacob wasn't so protective over Benjamin what they may have done to him in the effort to get rid of all of Rachel's children.

God can sustain anybody. He is a keeper. He is your High Tower. You can dwell under the shadow of the Almighty, under His wings. You can abide. God *kept* people in the time of famine, from time immemorial. Isaac had sown in the time of famine and reaped a hundredfold.

Now another famine had hit Israel.

We must know that God could have *kept* them in the time of famine if He had chosen to do so. Elijah was kept in the time of famine by a dirty bird. So the famine hit the land. God could have kept Jacob's kids—his whole family, during that time of famine. He could have kept them even while in Israel, but because their destiny was wrapped up in Joseph. They had to go to where Joseph was.

If these geniuses had killed Joseph, they would have killed all of their individual destinies. If Joseph had ended up dead for having been sold into Egypt, if God had not raised up another "Joseph", all of those destinies would have been lost as well. Reuben, Simeon, Levi, Judah… the Tribes of Israel would have not been, unless that God would have raised up other leaders. Witchcraft attempts to steal, kill and destroy the plans of God. We who are in the Kingdom are part of the plans of God. This is why God hates witchcraft so much and we see it is nothing to be played with. The plan of God, even though it is for individuals, it is also for all.

I bind the *spirit of selfishness* and selfish ambition, in the Name of Jesus.

That was not God just sustaining those brothers and their father; that was God sustaining the Tribes of Israel, all of them. That was God keeping covenant with Jacob – blessed him. That was God keeping covenant with Isaac. That was God, keeping covenant with Abraham, whom He had said, ***Through you*** **will all the nations of the Earth be blessed.**

Joseph wasn't your just any typical run-of-the-mill anybody. He was someone special to God. God could have chosen anyone, but he chose Joseph. You are not a typical run of the mill anyone; you are also *called* of God.

In order for Joseph to do what he had to do regarding those boys--, his evil brothers, he had to be related to them. These are the same guys that were going to kill him, the same ones who sold them into slavery, the same ones who lied to him and lied on him, lied to his father about him. They are the same ones who despised him and couldn't speak peaceably to him, yet Joseph had to end up being the helper to those boys. In order to do this, he had to be related to them.

Now you can see what's wrong with your family and what you have to do with the gift or the gifts that you have for your family. The giftings that you have, have to come through you, to them. And, it **has** to be you helping and praying for them, because you have to be *related* to them. There is a certain authority that we get because of being in the same bloodline. There are things you can pray for your siblings (and parents) that others have no authority to pray because they are not related to them.

You've heard of the Kinsman Redeemer from the Book of Ruth? You have to be kin to someone to be a kinsman redeemer. Maybe that's the why you're the only one (right now), in your family that's saved. Maybe that's why you're the only one who's delivered. Maybe that's why you're the only one that seems to have good sense or is going to church. It's you--, tag, you're it. You're it.

So why are they all messed up?

Because they are.

Why are you the only one that's delivered?

Because of the Grace of God.

You may be the only one who's standing in the gap for them. And you can because you have a certain authority because of being related to them.

They may not even know Jesus. You're the only one who's standing in the gap for them right now. You are their *acting* kinsman redeemer until our precious Redeemer can make atonement and grant them full salvation, in Jesus' Name.

You're related to them to lead them into their redemption with Christ Jesus, and their deliverance—or at least plant the seeds.

Why are they all messed up?

Because they are.

Why aren't you?

The Grace of God.

Envy

The historian, Josephus also said that envy in mankind is usually between them and their nearest relations. Especially they are jealous of the prosperity of their nearest relations. Have you envied your nearest relations? Perhaps they were in the gap to help you. Perhaps they were *sent* of God with gifts on board to come through them to help you. Or, perhaps you were the one sent to help them, but they envied you.

Touch not God's anointed, do His prophet no harm.

Who is His prophet?

Anyone He sends with a Word. Anyone he sends with anointing. Do you need to repent at this time? If you do, take your time and do it.

So, the brothers tried to demote Joseph spiritually, but **promotion** comes from the Lord.

Demotion, then, must come from the devil.

Promotion comes from the Lord. No one can demote you spiritually but you, yourself, by unrepented sin. No one, nowhere except God,

Who shall separate us from the love of Christ? shall tribulation, or distress, or persecution, or famine, or nakedness, or peril, or sword?

As it is written, For thy sake we are killed all the day long; we are accounted as sheep for the slaughter.Nay, in all these things we are more than conquerors through him that loved us. For I am persuaded, that neither death, nor life, nor angels, nor principalities, nor powers, nor things present, nor things to come,Nor height, nor depth, nor any other creature, shall be able to separate us from the love of God, which is in Christ Jesus our Lord. (Romans 8:35-39)

The gifts of God are given without repentance, so no one can demote you spiritually. Whatever God has planned for you to be spiritually is what you shall be, if you obey Him, listen to Him, obey, and matriculate in the things of the Spirit, as you should.

No one, no matter what they say about you, no matter what position they put on you, no matter what title they take from you or put on you, you are still whoever you are in the Lord.

I am that I am.

When Moses wanted to know from God, *Who shall I say, sent me?*

God replied, ***Tell them I am, that I am sent you.***

Well, if you are in Christ, then you *am*, that you am. You *am* (are) God says you am (are), in Jesus' Name.

No one can demote you outside of your own division, rebellion, disobedience, or sin. They couldn't even demote Joseph spiritually because the gifts and calling of God are without repentance.

The brothers wanted to say that Joseph was not what his dream said that he was. They thought that a flesh demotion would take care of Joseph. But Joseph was greater than that because of spiritual purpose. Truth was in his bowels as to whom he was. You see, there was such a great anointing in Joseph that all those trials and tribulations that he went through at the hands of those brothers and in Egypt could not squelch that anointing and destiny.

When you are strong in the Lord, no one can change your name. No one can change your title. No one can change your anointing. No one can change your position. No one can put a new label on you. If God says that you are something you see even in the dreams, you **are** that. If it is prophetic, you have to pray it through and walk in it to your destiny.

Bow to the Anointing

In Joseph's dreams, the family wasn't really bowing to Joseph, but Joseph was a boy then and that's what he thought. Further, his brothers had proved themselves carnal, so that's what they would have thought also. He didn't have sense enough to really know that they didn't know they were bowing to that ***anointing*** that God was to put in him. They were not really bowing to Joseph.

They were bowing to the authority of God for the purpose that God had given him.

Because of this truth can you now see how idolatry works? When people bow to or give obeisance to things, it is not really to the thing, it is to the invisible spiritual **power** that is represented by the natural, seen *thing*. For example, every time you place a gift under a Christmas tree or remove a gift from a Christmas tree you are bowing to the tree. The power behind the worship of Christmas trees is Baal. Do any of us really intend to worship or give worship to Baal?

So even in God's Kingdom the prophetic dream of the brothers bowing to the sheaves that represented Joseph was a representation of bowing to the anointing and the anointing was of God, so God would be getting the honor and the respect and the worship.

Not bowing to idols is why Mordecai didn't bow to Haman in the Book of Esther. Haman *represented* a false religion, or a false *god.*

This is why when the music was played, Daniel didn't bow to the statue that Nebuchadnezzar had set up. It would not be the statue that would get the worship, it is the power behind the statue, that would receive the worship.

Stop Being Shocked

Before Joseph went through the *University of Through*, he thought his family would be bowing to him. He did think it was about him, but he was a teenager; what do they know? So if someone is acknowledging or giving you honor, they are not bowing to you, sisters or brothers. They are not bowing to you. It's not about you. It's the God that's in you. They are bowing to the anointing and the authority that God has placed in you, that God allows to go *through* you. That is, unless your ego and pride try to capture God's worship for yourself. Saints with prospered souls know better than to try to touch God's worship and glory!

Yet, here is where men can fail. God showed Joseph those dreams and then God raised

Joseph up in such a way that GOD's anointing didn't go to Joseph's head.

Demonic anointing is sought after by those who want to be big, famous and rich—fast, and without God.

God's anointing is given by God to those whom He can trust, those who are His sons that He has raised up. It is given to those who have soul prosperity, so they don't get a big head when GOD's anointing works through them, and they get to live in the overflow.

Where men fail is when GOD's anointing works through them and they plow with God's heifer, as it were and turn it into great empires for themselves. It may not mean that they started out that way, but if they end up that way that is a loss of testimony to the Father, and for the Body of Christ.

Some do start out the wrong way, the demonic way. They do get anointing and power from the kingdom of darkness, and some masquerade as having gotten power from God. This is why we must discern every *spirit*. Every *spirit*.

Saints of God, please stop being shocked and surprised when someone who got their “powers” from the devil must pay up. As said, all didn’t start out that way, some truly get deceived and fall. But those who get certain fame, gifts, talents from the devil will have to at some time pay this piper. Usually, it is at a most visible and embarrassing time, for all the world to see and ridicule. When you see a person with so much and they are not handling it well—such as with certain celebrities, you can pretty much know that they didn’t get their “gifts” or “luck” from God. When they fall, and they will, stop being shocked.

God does not give us more than we can bear – to the negative or to the positive. More positive than we can bear or use gracefully is a negative. And, that is not from God.

If there is no Godly purpose to a thing, God will not anoint it. So if it is anointed and God didn’t do it—don’t be shocked at who did.

Purpose & Anointing

When purpose and anointing are at the center of the vision, then it's of God, and it's from God. Oh, but the Word says, *Touch not mine anointed do my prophets no harm.*

When seeing an anointed person near you, do not covet it; do not be jealous. Anointing that is associated with you in proximity to you, is probably *for* you. It's for you, directly or indirectly. So the anointing is for the unctionized gift that's in a person that God has put in the vessel that is in proximity to you. This person could spend time with you, sit on the pew with you, or they could work with you at the office. That anointing could be for you directly or indirectly.

Touch not mine anointed do my prophet no harm.

That anointing might be for you. You don't touch it. Don't harm that vessel. Even if it's not for you, it is too dangerous to touch what is God's.

You need to be interceding and praying that the person will deliver the gift that God is *sending by* them.

You need to intercede. This gift may be delivered to the person just on the other side of you because they need deliverance. And maybe because of their deliverance, they'll stop clowning and getting on your last nerve like they did last week. Or maybe they'll finally be set free from their bondages. What a joy that should be since that's your brother and your sister. Therefore, you should care.

Well, maybe they'll start flowing in their ministry and stop hindering yours. Maybe they'll begin to assist you in your purpose. We should be every joint fitly joined together, working together, not against one another.

Do God's prophets no harm. Further, he that receives a prophet receives the prophet's reward. You see, the reward is the gift that's *to* you and **<u>for</u>** you. Anointing this near you is probably for you, to bless you directly or indirectly. Intercede that FedEx the postmaster, and Brown will deliver. Intercede that the person will know how to deliver the gifts that they've been entrusted with.

If you're *near* some anointing, it is a gift for someone, and that someone could be you. If it's not you, either way-- don't touch it. Hands off.

They Rejected Jesus

So the brothers tried to demote Joseph. They touched that anointing. And they tried to move Joseph from the family, and physically they tried to demote him. But they couldn't do it. *Touch not God's anointed.*

The very same thing that those boys needed to preserve them and keep them alive was the very same thing they rejected.

But did the people not also reject Jesus? So don't feel bad when people scorn you, revile you, and reject you. Marvel not. They hate you. They hated Jesus first.

You got a gift on board. It's got a delivery anointing on it. Then you need to go forward with what you have, and deliver what God *sent by* you.

That Coat

What this book really is about though is that coat. That coat of Joseph's. They stripped Joseph out of his coat of many colors. They physically stripped him of his identity and family connection. Even though they couldn't demote him from the family, he was still Jacob's son. But they stripped him of his identity and his family connection, as far as the outside world could see.

What you wore in those days, said who you were, what kind of clothes you had on. The royals wore purple, and Joseph was raised by a man had been a supplanter, but his name had been changed to Israel, which means *prince*. Because what you wore in those days said who you were, so the brothers took off Joseph's coat. When strangers came along, none of the ten boys who were related to him would vouch for him. When the Ishmaelites or Midianites came by, and Joseph's brothers were selling him as a slave, no one said, *That's my brother*. even Reuben who had first said, *Don't kill him,* didn't because Judah got the bright idea to sell Joseph as a slave. Still, none of them said, *Hey, that's my brother.* They had to have acted as though they didn't know him.

People didn't have ID's back then. They didn't have a driver's license, a DMV card, fingerprinting, or DNA. Who was anybody?

In those days, you were whoever you said you were, as long as you had people to vouch for you, or at least one someone to vouch for you, confirming your identity.

Who Is My Brother?

When you go into spiritual warfare and intercession for another, you are vouching for your brother or your sister. When you do that spiritual work, you are saying, *Devil, get your hands off my brother. Get your hands off Brother So and So. Get your hands off sister so and so. I'm vouching for them because they're in my family and I'm going to stand here in the gap for them.* Even if it is a silent intercession or praying in the Spirit, you're vouching for that person's **identity**. You're saying that person is in my family; they are my brother, they are my sister.

You are saying, *Devil, you cannot sell them down the pike into slavery.* Selah.

You might have them in a pit right now. My brother or my sister may be going through, but no Ishmaelite, no Midianite can buy their soul. No one can buy them. No, I'm not willing.

No! Pharoah cannot have them.

Mrs. Potiphar cannot steal their sexual rites or drain virtue from them.

No, they cannot go to prison and stay locked up with the risk and threat of death over their life. That's my brother! That's my sister! As a matter of fact, take them out of that pit right now, in the Name of Jesus.

Saints of God, that is what you do when you intercede for others, you are identifying them as from the Kingdom of God, and the Household of Faith, you are bringing them out of the pit or any other trap or snare that the devil may have set for them.

Praise God.

Who Was Joseph?

Without his coat, and no one to confirm his identity, who was Joseph? There was no milk carton with his picture on it. But Joseph's identity was not removed from Joseph. Joseph did not forget who he was; neither did he forget his family. Who your family is, is part and parcel of who you are.

That is another common failure of men—the devil has them so entangled, so wrapped up for so long that they forget who they are, and the devil reprograms them for evil by first erasing or distorting their identity.

Thank God, the anointing, purpose, even the dreams in Joseph did not allow him to forget who he was.

When Joseph was sold into slavery, he was 17 years old. So by the time his brothers saw Joseph again, they didn't recognize him. Who would have recognized him?

How many of us have been sold into slavery, into the world and don't look like ourselves anymore? We need a spiritual somebody who's got at least one spiritual gift inside of them and anointing to use it, to recognize us and call us back to ourselves. We need someone that God has *sent* or *sent by* to identify us and remind us of our dreams and our visions that the Lord has given us to reacquaint us of our purpose and call us back. Thank you, Lord.

Women, if you are in a relationship that you never should have gotten into--, it's as though you are in slavery and bondage. Would anyone recognize you now? You may not recognize *yourself* right now. You may not even look like yourself anymore. You need more than a *physical* makeover, you need someone to deliver a spiritual gift to you, to remind you who you are, and what you came to this planet to do.

That anointing is what's going to get you out.

Saints of God, there's an anointing that's working through you. You need to stir it up or let the Word and your praise and worship stir up the gifts. Let the words of this book stir it up. If that is your need, I pray that the Lord will send someone to speak to the *spirit* that's in you--, to cast out all evil *spirits* and to impart and/or stir up the gift of the Holy Spirit that's in you, to get them out of every slavery and bondage situation.

That Coat & the Blood

When Joseph was stuck in the well, no one vouched for him. When he was sold into slavery; no one vouched for him. That is what is happening if you are not interceding for anyone; you are not identifying the Body of Christ. And, if no one is interceding for you, the same is happening to you.

Jealous brothers took Joseph's expensive coat from him, and now Joseph is in Egypt, wearing the coat of a slave.

Before he became a slave, Reuben said, *Don't kill him. But we'll take this coat. And we will use the blood of this wild animal, this goat. And we'll take this to dad and tell him that Joseph is dead.*

All the while, that coat, that symbolic coat of many colors with the colors that represented all kindreds and tongues and nations and cultures and groups of people **was dipped in the blood.**

It was in the blood: Hallelujah.

In the Old Testament, the blood of animals was what was used for atonement. We didn't have the Better Blood of Jesus yet. So that coat was covered by the blood. Hallelujah.

They took Joseph's coat from him. Now, in Egypt, he's wearing a different coat, a different outfit, the coat of a slave. Yet, Joseph became a successful slave.

Many of us used to be successful slaves to the world. But that doesn't mean you have to stay a slave just because you were good at it. God's Word says, that whatever you set your hands to is going to prosper. So many of us were successful slaves.

Since that time, since you've been called out of the world and delivered, what are you doing? What is your worship about? Where do you work? Are you doing what God has told you to do? Or, are you just doing something, just to be doing something?

While Joseph was in slavery, he had on the coat of a slave, but in a very absurd and perverse way, Mrs. Potiphar, took that coat of slavery off of Joseph. Joseph was serving in his house in an absurd way, Potiphar's wife helped Joseph by removing his false coat, his coat of slavery from him. She removed his false purpose, his false world, and she helped Joseph in a really strange way.

When Abimelech, a Philistine king, had Sarah in his palace, God punished that house by making them all barren until they released her. (Genesis 20).

Isaac and his wife, Rebecca also had a similar Abimelech interaction. (Genesis 26:8)

When Pharoah's captain had Joseph in his house, it was the same, because they all wanted sex from Abraham's bloodline.

None of the captors got it, though.

The child of a prince, captive by pharaoh, that's reason for retaliation, but Jacob thought Joseph was dead.

Sarah and Rebecca were rescued from each Abimelech before any sexual encounters. Joseph, their great grandson, and grandson, respectively, also did not have sex with any captor because he ran away from Mrs. Potiphar, leaving his slave coat.

This is not by happenstance. Sex forms deep, deep covenants that are breakable, but not always easy to break. I know people who have **for years** been breaking evil covenants because of the spiritual entanglements that make it so difficult to become extricated from. If you need to break these evil soul ties and entanglements because of illegal sex, do it now. Do it today because you don't know how long it will take.

Joseph, too, in a sense was captured and living in a palace where he did not belong. But after the Mrs. Potiphar events, even though Joseph made the right decision, he was punished in the natural.

You see, Joseph was a slave. He was supposed to do whatever that woman wanted, but religiously he could not do it. It was not something that would jibe with him. This wasn't something he could do.

Just because you work at a job doesn't mean you do what the job says for you to do, even if you are a slave to the money because of debt. Will you make the right decisions? Which is worse, losing position and favor with man, or losing position and favor with God? Which is worse, the punishment of man, or of God?

Let that anointing stir up in you, and let the anointing that's going through you, minister to others. God will allow you to live in the overflow of that anointing, and you move and have your being in that overflow of the spiritual you, you will make the right decisions and you will come out of that false coat because you are not a slave to mammon. You cannot serve 2 masters.

Not Prison

Joseph, who was a slave, was removed of that coat by Potiphar's wife, but at that time it looked bad for Joseph. It looked even worse because then Potiphar judged him, and he got a political and a natural demotion. First, he was an upstairs slave and now he's a downstairs slave, a prisoner. But he never got demoted spiritually because he was still whoever God says he was going to be; and Joseph remembered himself--, he remembered who he was.

Joseph then went to prison, and there he became a successful prisoner. But isn't it just like sin? At first, you're slave to something, and then you get in full bondage to it, and then you become a prisoner to it? First it seems like fun, and then it's not.

But meanwhile. There's famine in the land and the ten evil brothers are on their way to Egypt.

Back home with Jacob--, the coat, the original coat, the one that his father gave him, was dipped in the blood. It was the blood of an animal because as I said, we didn't have the Better Blood yet,

These brothers tried to kill Joseph without actually killing him, themselves. They were trying to get rid of him and trying to kick him out of the family and demote him spiritually. In all their scheming, they dipped the coat in the blood of the goat.

The Jews wanted Jesus dead, but they didn't want to kill Him themselves, so they found a way to get the Romans to do it. But, Jesus' garment was stained with His own Blood, the Better Blood.

Joseph's purpose, his identity, his future, and his destiny was covered by the blood, even though he wasn't *in* the coat.

In addition to that, Jacob's 10 boys made Heaven and Earth agree. They didn't even know about it yet. Because you see, without them having done that, Heaven and Earth would not have agreed because every kindred, every tongue, every culture, every nation was covered by the blood that was on that coat of many colors.

We thank You, Lord, for the Blood.

So even though the dad grieved, especially after probably hearing the story of his daddy Isaac, and Isaac's near sacrifice, how many times, he had to have grief in his heart over Joseph. They had to be thinking that they were under some type of a generational curse instead of a generational blessing.

But God is a keeper of Covenant and he promised Abraham, Isaac, and Jacob to bless them.

As Jacob, Joseph's daddy preserved the coat, also know that the gifts of God are without repentance.

You know your mom will keep your high school keepsakes, for how long? Your newspaper clippings till they turn yellow. But how much more will parents keep things of great spiritual value? How much more will your spiritual-minded father, or your spiritual father, keep things that belong to you? This coat had blood on it from an alleged wild animal. We do know that no other brother got it. It wasn't handed down to Benjamin or given to another son. It wasn't burned. It was kept under the blood.

Joseph's purpose was preserved because his being out of place was not by his own will. Conversely, Jonah rebelled by his own will, but God allowed the blood to cover Joseph, even though he wasn't in the coat. God will preserve those gifts because he loves the people that He's planning on sending the gifts that you have in you to--, as much as he loves you.

See, it's not all about you. It's about *through* you. The people who are going to be blessed, the nations and kindreds and the cultures, and the tongues that are going to be blessed *through* you. God loves them as much as He loves you, so God will preserve you to make sure that the others that you are assigned to will receive the gifts that He has *sent by* you. It is because those people *will*, at some designated time, accept salvation, come out from the Multitude, and serve the Lord.

There's your answer.

So Messed Up

Why are people like they are?

Why are they so out of order and ungodly, and unholy?

No one has delivered their gift to them yet.

How were the people in Ninevah acting before Jonah got there?

Bad. They needed their gifts; they needed repentance. Recall, like Jonah, sometimes humans think they have the right to withhold a gift, the Lord's gifts that flow through them. But that is not allowed. The Lord grieves when you are not walking in your purpose, your gifting, and your anointing. He's patient, but He will not always strive with man.

You Cannot Be Demoted

You cannot be demoted spiritually. You cannot be. Even if a person's not speaking peaceably to you, you still are who God says you are. Just don't receive it. When someone saying something about you that is not true and that is not of God, they cannot demote you. And if somebody's not speaking peaceably to you, they're calling you out of your name, why are you spending time with them? Why are you even subjecting your ears and your heart and your spirit man to such filth? Why?

Another Robe

And there was another daddy that had a robe for his boy, the Prodigal Son. When he returned home, his dad gave him a ring, a robe, position, and authority. The Prodigal had wandered off. Outside of blatant, unrepented of sin, you can't even demote yourself from the family of God. God won't let you. The Prodigal wandered off. He didn't get sold off; he went off willingly.

Joseph didn't. Joseph was tricked. He was deceived. He was hoodwinked. He was probably tied up and forced.

But the prodigal got his inheritance before his dad had even died, packed his bags, and left. But his daddy preserved his robe for him, and he's a natural daddy. How much more your Heavenly

Father? If your natural parents know how to give good gifts, how much more does your Father who is in Heaven?

It is because of the Lord’s great Love and Mercy for us that your robe, your spiritual robe awaits. What does your spiritual robe look like? Is it many colored? Is it striped or is it polka dot? Is it purple? What does it look like?

Well, it looks like your purpose. It looks like you're anointing. It looks like your position. It looks like the gifts that you have on board to give to people. That's what it looks like. And because of the Lord's love for you, your spiritual gift or gifts are given without repentance. Use them wisely.

Your robe awaits, and your spiritual gifts still need to be delivered to the others that God sends you to. Because of the Lord's love for the people that He's sending the gifts to, your robe awaits.

Because of the Blood, because of the Blood of Jesus, your robe awaits.

Because of the Lord's abundant Mercy, love, kindness, and long-suffering. Your robe awaits.

So, your Heavenly Father. The one who gave you your coat, your purpose, your calling, destiny, future, your gifts, and anointing--, the one who gave you everything, He is waiting and looking for you and calling you even if you're out of place, or if you've stepped out of place, or if you've been delayed, detained, or held up.

If you've been put in a well. If you've been put on slaves' clothes by the bondages of this world. If you've been misspoken of, if you have not been put in the right positions by man because he just didn't know who you were. He thought you were slave when you were a son of a prince, when you were son of a king, when you yourself are a prince.

Or if man puts you in a place where he thought you could serve him, perhaps as the steward of his house when you should have been steward over much, much more, but that man, that *Abimelech or that Potiphar* tried to peg your spiritual gifts for his own use.

But those gifts are for other people--, for the people that God was sending them to. They were not for the person who saw it in you first, or saw it in a perverse way in you first and coveted those virtues.

And so the Lord has preserved your coat, your mantle, because it's dipped in the Blood.

All of Joseph's destiny was preserved because his coat was under the blood. Remember, the colors represent not just Joseph but all the tribes of Israel. Even though Joseph suffered, he suffered for all; all the Tribes were under the blood.

Even in in your bondage or slavery or your sin or people, trying to kill your purpose, plead the Blood, the Blood of Jesus. Hallelujah.

Your Purpose

Don't take your purpose lightly, but don't think more of yourself than you ought to. Remember that everything that you do affects everybody, whether you know them or not.

The gifts were preserved.

Has the Lord given you a many-colored dream? As asked before, What does your spiritual coat look like? Who are you in the Spirit?

A good man leaves inheritance to his *children's* children. So the robe dipped in the blood represents that all the tribes were put under the blood as well because Joseph was sent in place to preserve them. The Lamb was slain before the foundation of the world--, only Heaven and Earth had to agree. Thank you, Reuben.

Thank you, brothers. Children of Jacob, thank you.

What the devil meant for harm, God turned it to our good.

You intended to harm me, but God intended it for good to accomplish what is now being done, the saving of many lives. (Genesis 50:20)

If He Forgives

For Joseph's shame, he got double. What the devil meant to his harm, God turned it to good. God can look at a mess and say look at this mess, but then God can say, but I can use it. Even if family members are turning on each other, or everybody in the family is turning on one, God may not say anything, but He can still use it as long as the person at the center of the plan understands *though you*.

God may say, ***I can still use him as long as the boy knows is not about him and he's not the center of the world. I can still use him, I can still use this situation as long as the boy understands #1,and #2, as aforementioned. As long as the boy forgives, I can still use him. I can still use this situation. I can turn it for good.***

Know that if God is using you in ministry He will bless you so much that you can live in the *overflow*. Listen, **not** live on the gifts, but in the *overflow.*

The Third Coat

Oh, but there was another coat. Yes, yet another coat. And the Word says, *And he was clothed in a vesture dipped in blood, and his name was called the Word of God.*

It is recounted in the Gospels that they also took Jesus' robes and divided the robes among themselves. They took Jesus's coat, but not His identity. He knew who He was from the foundation of the world.

In the beginning was the Word, and the Word was God, and the Word was with God.

They didn't take Jesus' authority, because God preserved His place for Him. And where is He now? Even though He first descended, He then ascended to the right hand of the Father.

They didn't take Jesus' power because He has all power within Him, the fullness of the Godhead.

They did not take His destiny or His position because they took His robe--, because of the Blood.

They didn't take His dominion or His power, his strength, not His riches because He is in riches right now, in Glory.

They did not and could not take His Majesty.

They only took His clothing.

Jesus knew who He was before the foundation of the world, even though there were no DNA or fingerprints back then, no DMV or ID cards or driver's licenses.

How could you tell that it was Jesus? You could tell this was Jesus by the way He loved you. By the way He loved you first. The Bible says that Jesus first loved us and He also gave us the commandment to love one another.

A new commandment I've given to you that you love one another as I have loved you, and that you also love one another. By this shall all men know that you are my disciples. If you have love one to another, (John 13:34-35).

By this shall all men know you are My disciples, if you have love one to another. By this shall all men know that you are My brothers, and you are my sisters, by the love you show one to another. Hallelujah. That is your identification. So if they take your coat, it doesn't matter.

If they change your title, it doesn't matter. If they change your position, it still doesn't matter as long as you remember who you are in Christ. They can't demote you from the family. Because if you've got love, as long as you've got love, God can still use you.

He can still use you to be a vessel possessing yourself in sanctification and honor and you can still be a vessel to take gifts and Spiritual Fruit as God *sends by* you to the people of all kindreds and nations and tongues.

The ID is love. Jesus' ID is love. By the way He first loved us. And we know those in the Kingdom by the fact that the brothers and the sisters love you. We know you are of Christ by the way you believe *prophetically* that brothers and sisters, even those who are not lovely right now and unlovable, even ugly ones *will* love you.

They can take your robes. They could take the cloak. They can take your identity, but if you can love, God can still use you. They can take your covering and your protection in the natural and your identity. As long as you have love, you'll still be under the Blood. As long as you have love.

You see, they took all of that from Jesus, but He still had love.

The Prodigal Son tried to give his position away by riotous living. But he still had love because his father loved him. And that love covered the multitude of the sins of the prodigal.

They took it all from Joseph. But he still had love. He still had love for his half-brothers, his full brother, Benjamin, and his father, Israel. Joseph had love and he had the other thing that God needed--, **forgiveness**. He forgave them.

Whomever will love, whomever has love, God can still use you. God will preserve your place in your position. Oh, your robe awaits. And your position and your authority, your honor -- even though you might not be ready right now, it all awaits you.

Whatever amazing gifts God *sends by* you to folks, everybody's not going to bow to you.

They're going to bow to that anointing. They're going to bow to the gifting. They're going to bow to the purpose. They're going to bow to the Spirit and the power of God. Because it's *through you*. It's not of you. It is not from you. It's through you. Your robe awaits, though.

The Spirit of the Lord God is upon me. If you have love and you can forgive, the Spirit of the Lord God is upon me to identify and re-identify who you are, who you are, what you are called here, to remind you of your dreams and your purpose. To remind you of what God has called you to. To remind you that you are more than a conqueror, to remind you that you are still all that God says you are. To remind you to **love** and to remind you to **forgive**.

Even if you are thinking, *I could have been much further along than this if they hadn't delayed me.* If they hadn't detained me. I could have been much further along if I hadn't gotten to that well, or that bondage situation, that slavery to sin or the world. If I hadn't have gotten into that *situation. If I just stayed on the path*---,

Can you forgive them? Can you forgive your brothers and your sisters? Can you forgive the brothers as Joseph had to do?

Can you forgive them?

You may still be complaining --*But if my father had just come to my rescue,*--

Can you forgive your father? In the natural? Can you forgive the father figure in the natural? Can you forgive authority figures, the pastors, can you forgive them?

Can you forgive God for not coming when you thought He should come? Because maybe you're still going through the *University of Through*, where you learn it's not all about you.

Perhaps God couldn't show up just yet because you had to recognize it ain't all about you. It's not about the deliverance that came when you walked in the room. No, the power of God came in. Perhaps it was *in* you. Perhaps you were the anointed vessel that was carrying it. But it's not about you.

Oh, I could have been so much further along than this. I could have been so much further along. Stop complaining, saints of God, your robe, awaits you. This book is to tell you your spiritual robe, the robe that looks like your purpose, the robe that looks like your people, the robe that looks like the people you're going to go minister to is waiting on <u>you</u>.

Some of you--, the people you should minister to are in your family. And that's why your ministry is not further along than it is. That's a word from the Lord. That's why your ministry is not further along than it is right now, says the Lord. Because you have not yet ministered to your families. That's your first level of stirring you up, getting you out of the bondage that you're in, out of the cycle you're in by breaking your family members out by the anointing from God, that you allow to flow *through* you.

Your family?

Maybe that's why they're all messed up. They are your training ground, because the Lord says He will teach your hand to war and your fingers to fight. Your family may need you to be in spiritual warfare.

Your robe awaits you, if you have love, your robe awaits you.

If you can forgive –, the robe, awaits you.

Even if you did it to yourself, if you can still go back now, **forgive yourself** and love yourself. If you made some poor choices and no one was calling you out of your name and no one was talking you into anything, no one was leading you down a bad path, in the natural. Even if you did it yourself, you can repent, and God will forgive you. Then, you can forgive yourself. If so, then God can still use this.

Let's Forgive

Thank You Jesus, Father, in the Name of Jesus. I forgive the brothers. I forgive the sisters.

I forgive Potiphar.

Lord, in the Name of Jesus. Potiphar who represents anyone who had authority over me, a father, or a spiritual father, a father figure, an Elder, a parent, or a parental figure.

Lord, in the Name of Jesus. I forgive them …. say their names out loud right now as you forgive them. Forgive them.

If you can forgive them. God can still use this situation, even if it looks like a mess.

Jesus had a PhD from the *University of Through.* He matriculated through *The University of Through* and graduated with All Honors.

I forgive Potiphar, in the Name of Jesus.

I forgive Potiphar's relatives and staff -- that's all the people who are in power and are related to Potiphar who were telling me, *Do this, do this, go here, go here, do that or the other.*

I forgive the jailer.

Even when you were in your deepest bondage. Forgive the people who kept you down there by saying, *hey, this is fun. Let's stay here. Let's keep doing these drugs and alcohol.*

Forgive them, in the Name of Jesus. They were doing the best that they knew how to do. Forgive God, your Father, if you believe that He didn't come to rescue you, as soon as you thought He should have.

I'll tell you right now, you weren't ready. If you were ready, God would have already been there. As they say, He may not come when you want him, but He's always right on time.

Forgive all of those people in the Name of Jesus, and repent yourself. Repent of not having on your own robe by your own doing or your own choices or discarding that robe, soiling it, losing it, or selling it.

Thank God for the Blood. You thank Him for the Blood because you have been covered by the Blood, even when you weren't in your spiritual purpose. Your spiritual purpose and spiritual destiny are covered by the Blood. God protects purpose and anointing, and those that *will* do the **will** of God, even if it's in the future.

You may have been delayed or detained, but no more, says the Lord. From this day forward, no one can call you other than what God says you are because of the Blood.

Let God be true and every man a liar.

OK, Brown and FedEx and the Postman, it's time to deliver gifts. Yeah, if you can love and you can forgive, you can still deliver. You can go deliver those spiritual gifts and those Fruits of the Spirit to those people that God says for you to give them to. To the ungodly, to the unlovely, to the unlovable, to ugly ones. The smelly ones. To any of them. Even the people who tried to kill you in the first place. Even the ones you're related to. Even the ones who hate you. You don't think Nineveh had love for Jonah, any more than Jonah had love for Ninevah, do you? If you can forgive them, if you still have love--, the *agape* love of God, then God can use it, then God can use it *through* you.

Through Joseph

The Word says, in you shall all the nations of the Earth be blessed.

Joseph was down in that well--, those were his grandfather's and his great grandfather's wells. Abraham had dug those wells, and Isaac had re-dug them. Those wells had brought prosperity to that bloodline, yet it was nearly the death of one of their descendants. Stuck in that well, it seemed to be an impossible situation for Joseph. But God knew that the *future Joseph* could love and forgive even what those brothers were doing to him as they ate the lunch that Joseph brought them.

Through Joseph all the tribes of Israel every nation and kindred and tongue and culture, was preserved as a posterity, and blessed.

Through you, Abraham, shall all the nations of the earth be blessed. Hallelujah through you, Abraham. Our God keeps Covenant.

As you now see, Abraham's *through* happened with his great grandson Joseph, four generations later. Through you.

Abraham had to go through the *University of Through* because it wasn't all about Abraham. That blessing that God promised didn't begin to show up until Joseph. Isaac had wife troubles and only two children, Jacob had a bunch of wives, and his boys were kind of wild, in my opinion. But God, who knows all, preserved these Tribes. Therefore, all of them, all those expensive *colors* were being preserved even in a time of famine in Israel.

<u>You</u> also are an heir of Abraham. *Through you*, Dear Reader, shall all the nations of the Earth be blessed. God keeps covenant.

Look at your coat, in the Spirit. Look at the colors. Look at the expense and the investment that God has made. Oh, look at the Blood. It's dipped in The Blood.

Through you the nations of the Earth may be blessed.

And because of The Blood, and by the love of Jesus Christ and the love you have for even the brothers and the sisters. And the forgiveness, they shall be blessed, and God shall be glorified.

Hallelujah. AMEN.

Dear Reader

Thank you for acquiring and reading this book. I pray that it has enlightened and strengthened you.

May the Lord break you out of every captivity. May He gather you in all places that you have been scattered.

And may He restore you *at least* sevenfold, all that you have lost and all that has been taken from you. Even ***time,*** as He restores the years. In the Name of Jesus, Amen.

Dr. Marlene Miles

Other books by this author

AK: The Adventures of the Agape Kid

AMONG SOME THIEVES

Ancestral Powers

Blindsided: *Has the Old Man Bewitched You?*

https://a.co/d/5O2fLLR

Churchzilla, The Wanna-Be, Supposed-to-be Bride of Christ

Demons Hate Questions

Devil Weapons: Unforgiveness, Bitterness,...

Dream Defilement

Don't Refuse Me, Lord (4 book series)

Every Evil Bird

Evil Touch

Fantasy Spirit Spouse

FAT Demons (The): *Breaking Demonic Curses*

The Fold (4 book series)

The Fold (Book 1)

Name Your Seed (Book 2)

The Poor Attitudes of Money (3)

Do Not Orphan Your Seed

got HEALING? Verses for Life

got LOVE? Verses for Life

got HOPE? Verses for Life

got money?

How to Dental Assist

How to Dental Assit2: Be Productive, Not Wasteful

Let Me Have A Dollar's Worth

Living for the NOW of God

Lose My Location https://a.co/d/crD6mV9

Man Safari, *The*

Marriage Ed. Rules of Engagement & Marriage

Made Perfect in Love

Motherboard (The)- soul prosperity series

Plantation Souls

Power Money: Nine Times the Tithe

The Power of Wealth *(forthcoming)*

Rules of Engagement & Marriage

Seasons of Grief

Seasons of War

Sift You Like Wheat

Soul Prosperity soul prosperity series 3

https://a.co/d/5p8YvCN

Souls Captivity soul prosperity series 2

The Spirit of Poverty

This Is NOT That: How to Keep Demons from Coming At You

Throne of Grace: Courtroom Prayer

Time Is of the Essence

Too Many Wives: *Why You Have Lady Problems*

Tormenting Spirits
https://a.co/d/dAogEJf

Triangular Power *(series)*

Powers Above

SUNBLOCK

Do Not Swear by the Moon

STARSTRUCK

Uncontested Doom

Upgrade: How to Get Out of Survival Mode

Toxic Souls (Book 2 of series)

Legacy (Book 3 of series)

Warfare Prayer Against Beauty Curses

Warfare Prayer Against Poverty

What Have You to Declare?

When the Devourer is Rebuked

The Wilderness Romance *(series)*

- *The Social Wilderness*
- *The Sexual Wilderness*
- *The Spiritual Wilderness*

www.ingramcontent.com/pod-product-compliance
Lightning Source LLC
LaVergne TN
LVHW011047110826
845149LV00015B/3389

* 9 7 8 1 9 6 3 1 6 4 1 5 2 *